YO-BSL-066

Francisco Pacheco   Courtesy of the Archives of the University of Santa Clara

FRANCISCO PACHECO
OF
PACHECO PASS

by

Dr. Albert Shumate

HOLT-ATHERTON PACIFIC CENTER
FOR WESTERN STUDIES
Monograph Number VII

Published by the University of the Pacific
Stockton, California
ISBN 0-931156-07-6

TABLE OF CONTENTS

ACKNOWLEDGEMENTS

The writing of this monograph has been greatly aided by the assistance of many wonderful persons. First and foremost, I would like to acknowledge my debt of gratitude to Ruth Teiser and Catherine Harroun for their special help. I also received valuable aid from Dr. Michael Mathes of the University of San Francisco, Mrs. Alfred (Amelie) Elkinton of Carmel Valley, and Betty Gardiner.

I also wish to extend special appreciation to Mr. and Mrs. Everett G. Hager for compiling the index.

I am greatly indebted to the following kind and considerate librarians and historians: James Abajian, Gary Kurutz, and M. K. Swingle of the California Historical Society Library, Dr. Ray Billington of the Huntington Library, Robert Becker and Leslie Shaw Clarke at The Bancroft Library, Ethel Crockett and Therese Lawrence of the State Library in Sacramento, and Dr. William N. Davis, Jr., at the State Archives.

I would like to thank for their valuable assistance: Harry Downie of the Carmel Mission, Gaylord H. Nelson of Salinas, Jack Brotherton of Modesto, Rev. Gerald McKevitt, S.J., of Santa Clara University, and Martha Seffer O'Bryon of the University of the Pacific.

Others who gave helpful assistance included: Clyde Arbuckle, Morley Baer, Dr. Dudley Bennett, Mrs. George Grunnagle of Tres Pinos, Mrs. Gerald Harrington, the Hawkins family of Hollister, Warren Howell, Roger Jobson, Mrs. Michael Kalend, Frank Latta, Richard Nason, Jr., Marjorie Pierce, Roger Rehm, Monserrat Roca, Madeleine Rose, Bartolome Sepulveda, James C. Voss, and Dr. R. Coke Wood.

Finally, I wish to express my debt to the late Ralph Millikin of Los Banos, a fine gentleman, and to the late Rev. Maynard Geiger, O.F.M., a great scholar.

FOREWORD

Thousands of motorists drive over Pacheco Pass, but few know anything about the sturdy pioneer, Francisco Pérez Pacheco, whose name it bears.

For many years I have collected information relating to Pacheco and his ranches, my interest having its origins in my admiration of Paula Fatjo, a worthy descendant of Pacheco, who still ranches on his land grant, the San Luis Gonzaga.

Like her ancestor, she raises horses and cattle, and here is located her famous Arabian horse farm. Her love for fine horses may well be part of her Spanish California heritage.

A graphic description of the Californian's affection for fine horses has been written by Lieutenant Joseph Warren Revere. This grandson of Paul Revere visited the "Rancho of Don Francisco Pacheco" and later wrote of the Californians:

> After his wife and children, the darling objects of a Californian's heart, are his horses. In this respect he is not surpassed by the Arab. His whole ambition centers in his horses; his livelihood depends on them, and they are the chief ministers of his pleasure . . . . The lineage of the California horse is undoubtedly of the purest and highest . . . all derive their descent from the Andalusian horse . . . pure Arabian descent. . . . I should know something of the Arabian horse, having seen and mounted the noblest of the race in the stables of Mohammed Ali, Viceroy of Egypt and his son Ibrahim Pasha.[1]

This short monograph salutes Francisco Pérez Pacheco and his descendants, California *rancheros*!

Feliciana Pacheco, wife of Francisco Pacheco

CHAPTER I

PACHECO PASS

Francisco Pérez Pacheco, for whom Pacheco Pass was named, is a relatively unknown California pioneer. He was not related to the well-known Governor Romualdo Pacheco or the Pacheco families of Contra Costa, Santa Clara, and Marin counties. His name, however, has been spoken more often than any of theirs, for the pass that bears it has, through the last century and a half, been one of California's major routes of travel.

Pacheco Pass is one of the few easy passages between the coast and the great Central Valley. Today, California State Highway 152, connecting Gilroy in Santa Clara County to Los Banos in Merced County, runs through this gap in the Coastal Range. The closest parallel passes lie a hundred miles to the north and the south. Not only is Pacheco Pass a convenient route for the people of the San Joaquin Valley and the Monterey, San Benito, Santa Cruz and southern Santa Clara regions, it also allows cooling breezes from the Pacific Ocean to flow into the Central Valley.

The earliest recorded name of the pass was San Luis Gonzaga, taken from the nearby creek. The saint's name was bestowed upon the creek by the explorer Gabriel Moraga, who "discovered" the pass (although Indians had traversed it for hundreds of years) on June 21, 1805, the feast day of San Luis Gonzaga.[2] His name, sometimes anglicized as St. Louis, became the predominant place name of the area and was later applied to the rancho encompassing it.

Moraga continued to use the pass in his travels between the coastal valley and the San Joaquin, and the San Luis water hole on the creek was considered briefly for the site of a mission.[3]

When Indians of the Central Valley began successfully raiding ranchos of the *Californios* living on the coast, they drove their stolen horses back to the San Joaquin Valley through the pass. To halt these depredations, Governor Manuel Micheltorena in 1843 proposed that a stockade be built on Pacheco Pass.[4] This was not erected, however, because the Pachecos constructed a sturdy adobe, with gun ports, which became the guardian of the east entrance of the pass.

Years later, two witnesses, Benito Díaz and Rafael Rodríguez, testifying in 1852 before the United States Court regarding the Rancho San Luis Gonzaga grant, told of Indians "from the Tulares" using Pacheco Pass for these raids.[5]

1

In 1843 the Pacheco family was granted the vast Rancho San Luis Gonzaga, which extended over the entire pass, and within a few years the pass was called by the rancho owner's name. It was regularly referred to as Pacheco Pass during the conquest of California by the United States, when such notable personages as Generals John Charles Frémont and Stephen W. Kearny and Captain John Sutter traveled across it.[6]

After the discovery of gold on January 24, 1848, other army officers crossed the pass on their way to the gold fields. These included the Military Governor of California, General Bennet Riley, and two future generals, Captain Henry Halleck and Major Edward R. S. Canby. Also Lieutenant George H. Derby ("The Veritable Squibob") reported on California topography. General Riley wrote in Derby's Report that Pacheco Pass was one of three routes by which supplies might be sent to the mines.[7]

When the thousands of Argonauts of 1849 arrived at the gold fields, a great demand for beef developed. To supply them, many *rancheros* drove their cattle along the coast to Pacheco Pass, then crossed over the pass and proceeded north from Rancho San Luis Gonzaga to Hill's Ferry on the San Joaquin River. Usually cattle buyers took over there, but at times the cattle drives continued all the way to the mining camps.

While many of the famous crossed this gap, as already noted, so did the infamous. According to Remi Nadeau, the legendary Joaquín Murieta crossed the pass in March 1853 and headed south; Captain Harry Love, in pursuit "on a cold trail," followed, arriving in San Juan Bautista on July 12.[8] Colonel L. A. Norton, who crossed Pacheco Pass in 1853, called it the "Robber's Pass." Norton believed he had encountered the survivors of Joaquín's band at the San Luis ranch.[9]

Another bandit associated with Pacheco Pass was the notorious outlaw Tiburcio Vásquez, who, in 1871, held up the Visalia stage at Soap Lake at the border of Pacheco's land grant.[10] Such robberies continued for many years on the pass. In May 1877 the stage from Gilroy to Los Banos was stopped by two masked men and the express box taken. This stage was probably the Roberts' and George's Telegraph Stage Line that left Gilroy after meeting the Southern Pacific Railroad train on its arrival from San Francisco. The stage's speed may be judged by the fact that it took eight hours to reach the "San Louis Ranch" headquarters on the east side of the pass, some 37 miles from Gilroy.[11]

In 1853, when gold was discoverd on the Kern River, another group of treasure seekers used the pass. The *San Francisco*

Weekly Chronicle carried advertisements claiming that Pacheco Pass was the shortest and cheapest stage route to the Kern River diggings. One noted gold seeker on his way to the Kern River was Andrew S. Hallidie, who later achieved lasting fame as the inventor of the cable car. "For the entire distance," he wrote of the trip, "with the exception of the Pueblo of San Jose there were neither towns, villages or settlements and but one ranch where there was any activity, the St. Louis Ranch on the south east side of the coast range, after passing over the Pacheco Pass."[12] This was, of course, Pacheco's Rancho San Luis Gonzaga.

Pacheco Pass was for fifty years, under consideration as a route for a railroad. As early as 1853, Captain Joe Walker suggested it in his report for a proposed trans-continental line.[13] In 1864, after completion of the San Francisco and San Jose Railroad (which had originally been incorporated as the Pacific and Atlantic Railroad), the directors planned to extend the line south to Gilroy, then across Pacheco Pass and on to connect with the transcontinental railroad. The *San Francisco Alta California* of September 13, 1865, commented favorably regarding this proposal, and in 1867 the plans were filed with the Secretary of the Interior. [14] Maps of the 1850s also indicate the interest in railroad crossing the pass. Examples showing this proposed transcontinental route are seen in Lieutenant R. H. Williamson's 1855 map, Lieutenant G. K. Warren's 1857 map, and Dixson's and Kasson's map of 1859;[15] no railroad was built, however.

While the plans for a railroad remained on paper, Andrew D. Firebaugh, for whom the town of Firebaugh was named, built a toll road over the pass in 1856-57. Shortly afterwards a tavern was built near the toll gate by William Hollenbeck.[16] After the United States survey in 1859 establishing the boundaries of Pacheco's Rancho San Luis Gonzaga, Firebaugh and Hollenbeck filed a protest asking that their improvements on the pass be excluded. However, their protest was denied.[17] Later, in the 1860s, Lafayette F. Bell bought the toll road, and the tavern became known as Bell's Station, still a popular spot on the highway. Firebaugh's toll road was superseded in 1878 when a county road was built.

In 1858, shortly after Firebaugh's road was completed, Pacheco Pass became a part of the first Overland Mail route, the famous Butterfield Transcontinental Stage Line. This stage route ran from Memphis to San Francisco through the southwestern United States. After leaving Yuma, it traversed the San Joaquin Valley to Pacheco Pass, with the San Luis Gon-

3

zaga ranch headquarters, referred to as "St. Louis" on the maps of that period, being one of the stage stops. The Butterfield Line became a casualty of the Civil War in 1861, and John Butterfield's dream was over. Although the line existed only three years, its fame remains. At the centennial celebration of the Butterfield Trail in 1958, the "San Louis" Station was probably the only station that was still owned by the same family that owned it in John Butterfield's time. The first telegraph line from San Francisco reached Los Angeles in 1860. This line erected by the Pacific and Atlantic Telegraph Company followed the Butterfield Route and crossed the Pacheco Pass in 1859.

A correspondent for the *New York Herald*, Waterman L. Ormsby, was the only through passenger on the Overland Mail Company's first west-bound stage. He wrote of crossing Pacheco Pass: "Our road led immediately on the brink of many a precipice, over which a balky horse or a broken axle or an inexperienced driver might send us whirling in the air in a moment."[18] Since the date of that first stage ride one hundred and nineteen years ago, traffic has vastly increased. Today, Pacheco Pass is one of the heavily traveled highways of the state, but the western section of the road, as in Ormsby's day, is still dangerous and a disgrace to the California highway system.[19]

The road still traverses an unspoiled region, a region described beautifully by John Muir:

> The scenery . . . and all of nature in the Pass is fairly enchanting. Strange and beautiful mountain ferns are there, low in dark cañons and high upon rocky sunlit peaks, banks of blooming shrubs, and sprinklings and gatherings of garmet flowers precious and pure as ever enjoyed the sweets of a mountain home.[20]

Let us hope the great naturalist's words will always apply to this beautiful, rugged pass.

CHAPTER II
ARRIVAL IN CALIFORNIA

Francisco Pérez Pacheco was a Mexican by birth. He arrived in California in 1819 or 1820. As an artisan, he found himself in a social stratum inferior to the upper class, native-born *Californios*, most of whom were the sons of military officers or governmental officials and considered themselves leaders in Mexican California. Through constant hard work, however, Pacheco became one of the region's wealthiest *rancheros*; even more remarkable, he retained his wealth after California became part of the United States, when most of the *Californios* lost their lands.

Pacheco was born in 1790 at Guadalajara, in what was then New Spain. He married Feliciana Gonzáles y Torres, a native of Toluca. She was the daughter of José Theodoro Gonzáles (sometimes spelled in the records González) and Francisca Torres. Feliciana was said to be "a descendant of one of the Aztec [*sic*] chiefs of the Valley of Mexico."[21]

It is not known for certain whether Pacheco arrived in California in 1819 or in 1820. Bancroft, in his *Pioneer Register*, reported that he "came with the artillery detachment under Ramírez in 1819."[22] But the same writer stated in another volume of his *History of California*, "I think the detachment of artillery about twenty strong, including a few artisans, under Sub-Lieutenant José Ramírez, must have arrived this year [1820] perhaps in the *Cleopatra* which arrived at Monterey on May 7, though there is no positive record to that effect."[23]

In the baptismal records at the Royal Presidio Chapel, the present San Carlos Cathedral, in Monterey is an entry of May 18, 1820, stating that Isidoro de la Santísima Trinidad, son of Francisco and Feliciana, "was recently born and baptized by the ship's chaplain of the Frigate *Cleopatra*, Father Manuel Gómez, of the Mercedarian order." (The Mercedarians were members of the Order of Our Lady of Mercy.) The entry continues that the Pachecos "recently arrived at Monterey with the fore mentioned Frigate which anchored in the Port on the sixth day of this month."[24]

The Pachecos, however, always declared that the year of their arrival was 1819. They did so in several subsequent baptismal entries, in Pacheco's wife's will signed in 1854,[25] and in the United States Courts. Pacheco, when applying for a land grant in 1826, wrote: "That in the year of 1819, the then Governor of the Territory ordered the petitioner . . . should construct gun carriages . . . ."[26]

Bancroft, quoting the Provincial State Papers, wrote that Sub-Lieutenant Ramírez and his men left Mexico in May 1819 for California by way of Durango, Guaymas, and Loreto in Baja Lower California and arrived in California the same year.[27] It is probable that if the Pachecos were in Baja California in 1819, they would consider themselves to be in California; Spain made little distinction.

In Bancroft's *Pioneer Register*, Pacheco's occupation is listed as "carriage maker,"[28] a term which has led to confusion. The *Alta California* on May 4, 1860, declared that Pacheco "worked for a long time at his trade of wagon making." Actually, horse-drawn carriages were unkown, or nearly so, in California in 1819. Pacheco, as he explained in his petition for the Rancho Los Turlarcitos in 1826, "constructed gun carriages and other things required in the artillery service" from 1819 to 1821 "when the work ceased."[29] Amelie Elkinton's article "A Monterey Expedition Against Rebel Indians" tells how, as the expedition was returning in 1824, a gun carriage broke near Jolón. It was taken on to La Soledad "where, by good fortune, the carriage maker and artisan Francisco Pérez Pacheco had put up for the night." After several days' work he was able to repair the broken carriage.[30]

In the baptismal records of his children born in the early 1820s, Pacheco is referred to as a "master worker" and as of the "Maestranza del Rey," a term Professor Michael Mathes defines as a master shipwright and artisan in the King's service. Juan Alvarado, testifying many years later in a land title case in a Federal Court, referred to Pacheco as "an overseer of workmen." Also in the same case he was called a "workman in the artillery corps."

There are no contemporary accounts or family tradition to verify the legend that Pacheco arrived in Monterey "a political prisoner" who made the voyage in chains.[31] While the period was one of tumult in Mexico, which was on the verge of its independence, Spanish reports were detailed, and the arrival of a political prisoner should have been noted. It was not. Apparently the earliest mention of Pacheco's arriving "in irons" is a statement Fernando Zanetta of San Juan Bautista made in 1928, over one hundred years after Pacheco's arrival![32] In fact, Zanetta was only five years old when Pacheco died![33] On the other hand, a rather glorified interpretation was given by Pacheco's son-in-law, Mariano Malarín, who stated his father-in-law came to California "to examine the forts and fix them up."[34] The truth apparently lay somewhere in between.

Pacheco's life in California commenced in a humble manner; he worked hard, however, and attained great material success in the land of his adoption.

Casa Pacheco, Monterey, California

CHAPTER III
THE INDIANS' REVOLT AND THE 1820s

Brave action during an Indian revolt in 1824 brought Pacheco his first measure of prestige. On February 21, 1824, Indians at the Missions Santa Inés and Purísima revolted. The uprising spread to Santa Bárbara Mission, but order was quickly restored there; however, at Purísima the Indians were successful and captured the mission.[35]

When tidings of this outbreak reached Monterey, the governor organized troops to quell the uprising. One hundred men under the leadership of Mariano Estrada and Francisco de Haro rode south to Purísima; the mission was recaptured and the revolt crushed. In his official report, Estrada stated that he "especially commends the valor of the artisan Francisco Pacheco who volunteered, acted as an aid and did good service with a gun."[36] As a reward for his service, Pacheco was commissioned brevet *Alférez*, a title comparable to ensign.[37]

In 1825 Governor Luis Antonio Argüello granted a town lot in Monterey to Pacheco,[38] who later made application for another lot a few blocks away for the purpose of obtaining better water. In 1849 he sold this lot, perhaps, as the Monterey historian Amelie Elkinton believes, because he either developed a better well elsewhere or used the large town well in front of the Cooper residence.[39]

On November 6, 1826, Pacheco petitioned, as an ensign in the army and resident of the Presidio of Monterey, for a tract of land which he claimed was vacant. It lay between Missions Soledad and San Carlos, and was known as Los Tularcitos. In his application he explained that he had brought his family to California in 1819 and found it necessary, in a strange country and without relatives, "to seek means of substance." He further stated that he now had a hundred head of cattle and a band of horses and mules but had no place to put them.[40]

A month later, on December 18, 1826, the former president of the California missions, Father Vicente Francisco Sarría, replied from Mission San Carlos, vigorously opposing Pacheco's petition. In a lengthly document he declared the land in question was not vacant but belonged to and was used by the Indians of the San Carlos Mission.[41] The governor, José María de Echeandía, did not grant Pacheco's request.[42]

In spite of his failure to acquire a ranch, Pacheco gradually established himself as a man of substance. It is not surprising that in 1828, when regulations from Mexico City called for the establishment of a *junta* of electors, Pacheco was selected as one of the five provisional members "who lived in or near the capital and could be depended on."[43] The following year he was holding another official position, *commandante* of the guard of the Monterey customs house.[44]

In this same year, 1829, Joaquín Solís led a revolt against Governor Echeandía and obtained control of Monterey. When Solís marched southward, he asked Francisco Pacheco to take command of Monterey; however, Pacheco wrote Solís that while he was willing to serve his country in any possible way, he "was not capable of undertaking the command, having neither the talent nor disposition for it."[45] Pacheco's reply was wise, as the revolt collapsed and Solís and some of his followers were sent to Mexico in irons.

Pacheco's family increased during the 1820s. When he arrived in California, he brought with him two children, Jacinta and Ponciana. The latter died April 23, 1821. Isidoro, already mentioned, was born in California in 1820, and then followed Carlos de la Trinidad, baptized on November 4, 1821; María Encarnación Teodora, baptized on April 2, 1826; María Isidora, baptized on January 4, 1829; and Antonio Julián, baptized on December 21, 1830.[46] In the "Padrón de las Familias del Cuartel de Monterey" There is also listed a son, Juan. Bancroft, in his *Pioneer Register*, shows 1823 as the date of his birth.[47]

It is of interest that after 1824 Pacheco is no longer referred to in the records as a "master worker" or similar designation but as "Don Francisco Pérez Pacheco."[48] The first decade in the new land, California, had not only brought Pacheco favorable recognition but also a notable increase in his family.

CHAPTER IV
A *RANCHERO* AT LAST!
THE 1830s

In the decade of the 1830s Francisco Pacheco continued to serve in official capacities. His positions were listed by Bancroft. In 1830 he was still, as in 1829, *commandante* of the *Resguardo* (home guard), and in 1832 he was acting *guardia* without pay. In 1834 he was again *commandante* of the guard and was also serving as *Juez de Campo* (rural judge in ranching matters). In 1833 he was treasurer of Monterey, and in 1835 a *regidor* (alderman). In 1832 Pacheco was called into military service as an ensign, along with Ensign Juan Malarín and Lieutenant Mariano Estrada, both to become relatives of his by marriage years later.[49]

In 1831 Pacheco became involved, in spite of himself, in the continuing political tumult of the time. As a result of a revolt in Southern California against Governor Manuel Victoria, which led to the governor's departure from California, Agustín V. Zamorano had full possession of the government.[50] On February 1, 1832, Zamorano, in his capacity as acting governor, called a council of war. Attending the meeting was Pacheco, referred to as "Citizen Francisco Pacheco, retired ensign in the Army." Pacheco signed Zamorano's report, the "Zamorano Manifesto," which preserved the legitimate government but, as Zamorano's biographer explained, "incurred, as Victoria before him, the undying enmity of those young native Californians who had become inoculated with extreme philosophies."[51] Pacheco never attached himself to the young ultra-liberal native Californians in their various schemes.

In 1835 José Antonio Carrillo persuaded the Mexican National Congress to pass a decree declaring that Los Angeles rather than Monterey would in the future be the capital of California. Monterey received the news with dismay, and William Hartnell and Francisco Pacheco were appointed to prepare a protest. One of their statements justifying Monterey's superiority as a capital read: "Here women, plants and useful animals are very productive."[52] At least women were placed first!

In the early 1830s Pacheco continued in his efforts to obtain land. Since his first petition for a land grant in 1826 conditions had changed drastically in California. There were only fifty private ranches in California in 1830, the year Governor José María Echeandía promulgated a law which provided for the gradual secularization of the missions. In 1833 the Mexican government issued several laws insisting on secularization.[53] The more liberal policies, which in effect transferred land from the missions to the settlers, resulted in an increase to over eight hundred grants by the time the Treaty of Guadalupe Hidalgo was signed in 1848.[54]

Regardless of this increase in ranch grants and the diminishing influence of the Franciscans, Pacheco in his second petition for land obtained the backing of the mission fathers which he had not enjoyed earlier. Father Felipe Arroyo of San Juan Bautista Mission wrote in support that the land was "not needed" and further "that it was not much used."[55] According to Father Maynard Geiger, O.F.M., this padre's "missionary work at San Juan Bautista is almost coextensive with the history of the Mission."[56] He served there from 1808 to the end of 1832 and from time to time visited the pools of water above the present Menjoulet Canyon, which became known as the Los Baños del Padre Arroyo.[57] (Years later this name was selected for the trading post that has grown to be the city of Los Banos.)

In this petition Pacheco recalled his military service and included statements of witnesses as to his good character. He also explained that his livestock herd had increased to 1,000 head of cattle and three bands (manadas) of horses. Further, his family had increased: he now had three daughters and three sons. (Apparently his son Carlos de la Trinidad had died before 1833.)

Pacheco asked for the lands known as Ausaymus,[58] including a section known as the Cañada de los Osos, its name recalling the numerous grizzly bears once inhabiting the coast range.[59] As late as 1862, William Brewer reported an encounter with a grizzley bear on the Pacheco Pass. The mission fathers had called this area San Felipe; Pacheco, however, often referred to the ranch as San Felipe de Guadalajara, honoring the city of his birth. The recorded name is the Rancho Ausaymus y San Felipe. The Committee on Vacant Lands reported these lands to be "not irrigable, but adapted to sowing and grazing."

In 1833 Pacheco's dream of owning a rancho became a reality at last when, on November 26, Governor José Figueroa granted him a part of the Rancho Ausaymus y San Felipe, which had belonged to Mission San Juan Bautista.[60] These ranch lands, consisting of two square leagues (8,870 acres), were located to the east of the present town of Gilroy, with San Felipe Lake (Soap Lake) on their western border, San Juan Bautista to the southwest, and the mountains forming the eastern boundary.

Pacheco then petitioned for additional land on the basis that the first grant was "too small and insufficient" for the stock belonging to him. Governor Nicolás Gutíérrez complied, granting an additional 8,870 acres on February 6, 1836.[61] Pacheco continued thereafter to enlarge this ranch through additional grants until it contained 35,504 acres, and this acreage was eventually confirmed by the United States Courts.[62]

In descriptions of the ranch, references are made to the Laguna San Felipe, locally known as Soap Lake because it was long the source of an important ingredient of soap. Lieutenant George Peard, R.N., of His Majesty's Ship *Blossom*, who was in California 1826-1827, wrote that "some soap is made . . . from a 'salt' . . . found on the edges of a lake near the Mission of San Juan."[63]

Pacheco made use of Soap Lake. In the late 1830s and throughout the 1840s he sold soap to Thomas O. Larkin. Numerous entries in the Larkin account books at the Bancroft Library refer to Pacheco's soap, and in April 1843 Larkin wrote Pacheco complaining of the quality of a shipment he had just received.[64]

In 1836 Governor Mariano Chico was expelled by the *Californios*, and several months later a leader of the revolt, Juan Bautista Alvarado, became governor. The native-born Californians were always suspicious of the Mexican-born Californians, and this may have influenced General Mariano Vallejo, Governor Alvarado's uncle, in his belief that Pacheco was plotting against the governor. Vallejo ordered a squad led by William Robert Garner, and including Mariano Castro, to arrest Pacheco. On February, 14, 1837, they arrived at Pacheco's ranch and arrested him and several others.[65] (A year later he had another unpleasant visit when his ranch was raided by Indians from the San Joaquin Valley.)

The details are scanty, but it is doubtful that Pacheco was involved in a plot. As already stated, he usually remained aloof from the politics of this confused period. Governor Alvarado must have realized Pacheco's innocence, for on October 14, 1840, he granted him another ranch, adjacent to his San Felipe Rancho.[66] This Bolsa de San Felipe was so called because it was a "pocket" nearly enclosed by a swamp, a willow grove, and a ravine known as Sanjón de Tesquisquite.[67] The Bolsa was also former mission land and consisted of 6,795 acres. Some mission Indians still lived there, and Pacheco allowed them to stay.

Pacheco's headquarters were located near the creek that bears his name, seven miles north of the present city of Hollister. In the United States Court hearings confirming his land grants, his ranch house was described as an adobe structure valued at $15,000. It was also stated that he had corrals for 200 head of horses and cattle and twelve cabins for Indians. The decade ended with Pacheco a *ranchero* at last, the owner of 42,299 acres of choice land.

Mariano Malarín, son-in-law of Francisco Pacheco

CHAPTER V
THE SPLENDID BUT NOT IDLE FORTIES
THE 1840s

Gertrude Atherton, creator of California legends, wrote a popular book at the turn of the twentieth century entitled *The Splendid Idle Forties*. The romantics have accepted this as characterizing California during the period "before the Gringo came." For Francisco Pacheco it may well have been a splendid era, but it was never an idle one.

In 1843 Pacheco's son Juan became the owner of a rancho adjacent to his father's. It was the vast Rancho San Luis Gonzaga, named for the creek so designated, as already mentioned, by Gabriel Moraga on his 1805 expedition. The Rancho San Luis Gonzaga had been granted to Francisco José Rivera two years before, but he failed to comply with Mexican law requiring that a house be built within the year and that he inhabit the ranch. In fact, by 1843 Rivera had left California, and two years had elapsed "without any news of the whereabouts of that individual."[68]

Thus on September 26, 1843, Captain José María Mejía of the Battallón Fijo de Californias, and Juan Pérez Pacheco, son of Francisco Pacheco, applied for this land, stating their occupation of it would "aid the defense against hostile Indians." In October 1843 the lands were declared eligible for re-granting, and Governor Micheltorena granted them to Mejía and Pacheco on November 4th of that year.[69]

The boundaries were as usual rather vague and included the rancho of Francisco Pacheco, the Baths of Padre Arroyo, the San Joaquin River, and the "territory of the wild Indians." The total area was 11 leagues, 48,821 acres. Three days after the grant had been made, Mejía conveyed his half interest to Pacheco; thus it would appear that Mejía's name had been used because of his close association with the governor. A year later Micheltorena, under attack by the *Californios*, sent Captain Mejía to Mexico to obtain aid,[70] but Mejía did not return to California and thus fades from the story.

Young Pacheco built a one-story adobe house on the east side of the pass at the San Luis water hole, said to have been the site of a prehistoric Indian village.[71] The construction of the adobe, with its gun ports for shooting, indicates the threat of Indian attack was indeed real. Miss Paula Fatjo, a fifth-generation descendant of Pacheco, restored this adobe for her home in 1948; however, this part of the ranch was chosen as the site of the San Luis Dam, a part of the Central Valley Water Project. In 1962

Miss Fatjo attempted to move the historic adobe to the top of the pass, her new homesite, but the building collapsed during transit. The ruins of the oldest home in the San Joaquin Valley are now at the new ranch headquarters on the site of the old Mountain House, and the former extensive pasture lands and beautiful stables are covered by the water of the reservoir. Certain sections of the population may be aided by land condemnation, but often the unhappy consequences affecting the individual are disregarded and quickly forgotten.

Francisco Pacheco continued to enlarge his domain. On July 26, 1844, he bought from José Castro the 33,690-acre Rancho San Justo. It had been granted to Castro in 1839 by his relative Governor Juan Bautista Alvarado. Pacheco paid Castro in kind: 200 young cattle valued at $6 per head, 200 calves at $3 per head, and $200 in produce, in all, $2,000.[72] As this property adjoined Pacheco's lands, the size of his ranch was greatly increased.

On July 18, 1841, Pacheco's daughter Jacinta, a troublesome member of his family, married Sebastián Núñez, a native of San Miguel el Grande (now San Miguel Allende), Mexico.[73] Núñez is listed as living at the Pacheco Monterey home as early as 1836. At the time of the marriage he was 43 years old, while Jacinta was 33. Little more than five years later, in November 1846, Jacinta died.[74]

Núñez remained in California. With the aid of his father-in-law he had been granted Rancho Orestimba on February 22, 1844. This ranch was on the west side of the San Joaquin River and consisted of 26,660 acres.[75] Located in the present Stanislaus and Merced counties, it extended from near Crows Landing at the north to the Pacheco lands which it adjoined at the south.

The Pacheco family ranch lands now consisted of over 150,000 acres. The Rancho San Luis Gonzaga at that time was larger than the grant later approved by the courts. It extended much farther to the east and to the north, in the latter direction to the border of the Rancho Orestimba. Evidence of the extent of the land then claimed is indicated by the small adobes erected by Pacheco east of the boundary that was later established by the United States Courts. North of Los Banos, a city built on Pacheco land of Mexican days, a Pacheco-built adobe still stands, the San Luis Camp adobe. In 1967 a commemorative plaque was placed on this building by the Native Sons of the Golden West. There was another one-room adobe, built by Pacheco, known as the *Cen-*

tinela (the Sentinel); it was also found by the United States surveyors to be beyond the official boundaries of the San Luis Gonzaga ranch.[76]

Francisco Pacheco's activities were not entirely devoted to the management and enlargement of his lands. Records of purchases which he made from Thomas Larkin indicate that from time to time he bought luxury items such as beads, guitars, and barrels of brandy! More prosaic was his purchase in 1847 of fifty pounds of cod fish! Often Larkin sold him velvet, linen and *marta* (cotton cloth), and woolen blankets.[77] The account books also show that Pacheco sold to Larkin "produce" and, as already mentioned, soap.

The political intrigue which plagued California at this time led to a revolt by the *Californios* in 1845 against Governor Micheltorena. Captain John Sutter's forces, aiding the harried governor, seized Manuel Castro, one of the leaders of the insurrection, and camped at the top of Pacheco Pass.[78] There Sutter's company was completely duped by a small band of *Californios* who, while greatly outnumbered, nevertheless obtained the release of Castro.[79]

In that same year, Captain Sutter wrote Pacheco from "Nueva Helvecia" asking for "800 to 1,000 head of steers." In return he promised to supply shoes, spurs, iron implements, hides of beaver, etc.[80] Sutter stated he needed the cattle to pay a debt to Antonio Suñol. It is not known whether Pacheco complied with Sutter's request, but as Pacheco was astute, it is doubtful; Sutter was known for his cavalier attitude regarding debts.

California's history in the 1840s was marked not only by internal political disturbances but, more significantly, by the increasing presence of United States citizens. In 1844 Governor Micheltorena attempted to develop a defense against the encroachments of the Americans. Plans were formulated to establish armed companies in certain areas, one being San Juan Bautista where Pacheco was appointed to be in charge of the *defensores de la patria*, consisting of a corps of cavalry. War stores were transferred to San Juan, but these arms were seized by the rebels already mentioned,[81] and that, it appears, ended Pacheco's involvement in military affairs.

With continual internal disorder and the increasing Indian threat, many became convinced that the United States flag would eventually fly over California, and with it would come a more secure and peaceful life. Thomas Larkin, the "first and last" American consul in California, wrote from Monterey in July 1846 a lengthy description of the prominent men of California. This appraisal was sent to James Buchanan, then Secretary of State, later to be President of the United States. Larkin was quite outspoken, quite severe in his criticism of many of the *Californios*, but regarding Francisco Pacheco he wrote in a complimentary manner: "From Mexico . . . large landed property and cattle . . . of much note and character." Regarding Pacheco's views Larkin wrote, "not having any hope of protection from the President [of Mexico], nor affection for the native government of California [he] would have his interests and views advanced by admission into the Union."[82]

Bernard DeVoto has referred to 1846 as the "Year of Decision." To Pacheco it must have been, for he appears to have cast his lot with the United States' interests. A principal figure in the conquest of California was John Charles Frémont, and on the eve of hostilities he and his men found themselves on Gavilán Peak overlooking San Juan Bautista, surrounded by *Californios*. No blood was shed, however, and Frémont continued on via Pacheco Pass into the San Joaquin Valley.

A few months later, in July, Frémont was again at the pass. Thomas S. Martin, who was with him, has told how Pacheco informed them that General José Castro and his troops were at San Juan Bautista. Frémont, prepared for combat, continued on to San Juan only to find Castro had departed for Southern California.[83]

Still another account indicates Pacheco's pro-United States attitude. California's first newspaper, *The Californian*, published in Monterey, reported on December 25, 1846, that Frémont gave the ranchers horses to carry on their business, and to "Don Francisco Pacheco, a Mexican gentleman, who had done everything in his power to forward the American cause he sent upward ninety horses." Then, "two or three days after Colonel Frémont had left these horses . . . the Indians from the Tulares . . . came down and swept off every horse they could find." The article concluded with: "When will the Californians come to their senses?"

William Garner also wrote about this raid on Pacheco's ranch: "This gentleman is owner of about thirteen or fourteen thousand head of cattle, and is now left without one horse to gather them with. What an immense loss he will have to suffer if the war continues six months longer!"[84]

Another who saw the Pacheco ranch was Captain Daniel D. Heustis, who in 1845 stopped in California on his way back to New England. He had been held a prisoner in Tasmania for his participation in a rebellion in Canada. Heustis wrote that he was "encamped on the ranche [sic] of a Spaniard named Perchuquea [Pacheco] who has the greatest herd of cattle of any man in California at the present time."[85]

William Heath Davis, in his account of California before the Gold Rush, included Pacheco in his "list of solid men." Davis noted: "Ranchos San Felipe and San Luis Gonzaga, about 40,000 acres of land; 20,000 cattle, 500 horses and mares, and 15,000 sheep. That rich hacendado was a large buyer of merchandise, and I sold many goods to him in 1844-1845."[86]

In November 1847 the surveyor Chester S. Lyman visited Pacheco's ranch. Later, having returned to the East where he became a professor at Yale University, he wrote about it. The home, he stated, was "a large two story house and for a Californian tolerably furnished. There being no chimney the room was warmed in the eve by a dish of coals. The old gentleman we found kind and hospitable." Lyman stayed overnight and left the next day, after a breakfast of "beef and beans . . . having made a partial arrangement to survey his ranch which consists of 36 square leagues" (150,000 acres).[87] Unfortunately for Pacheco, Lyman never returned and no survey was made.

A description of Pacheco's adobe ranch house was written many years later by Chester G. Gillespie, who lived in it from 1889 to 1894. He described it as being two stories, long and narrow, and containing twenty-two rooms. Broad verandas extended the full length of the house, both front and rear. The building had a large attic for storage, and the roof was shingled in redwood cut in the Santa Cruz mountains. Gillespie claimed that during the 1906 earthquake large parts of the three-foot-thick walls collapsed.[88]

Pacheco's ranch land was mentioned by Etienne Derbec in a letter written from Agua Fría, May 9, 1850: "Before the discovery of the mines, Rancho Pacheco was the end of the inhabited country." Here Derbec, on his way to the Mariposa gold fields, replenished his supplies and "started into the California mountains."[89]

In 1847 Thomas Larkin received a commission from the President of the United States as Naval Agent for the Northwest Coast of America. He asked "my oldest friends in this country" to sign a bond for $30,000. These friends were "Don Francisco Pacheco, Don M. G. Vallejo, Don Salvador Vallejo and Jacob Leese," an illustrious group. In his letter to Pacheco he asked him to sign as one of the "four principal men of property in California." Pacheco signed on October 18, 1847, in the presence of Walter Colton, the *alcalde* of Monterey. One more name was added later to the Larkin bond, that of William A. Leidesdorff.[90]

With the war over, his lands protected by the Treaty of Guadalupe Hidalgo, and the Indian threat a thing of the past, Pacheco undoubtedly anticipated years in which he could continue to improve his enormous holdings peacefully. However, a few days before the signing of the treaty, far to the north at Sutter's mill on the American River, James Marshall had made the discovery which changed not only California but all the nation.

When the vast multitude of gold seekers arrived in California, the demand for beef, as already mentioned was great. Pacheco was able to sell at greatly inflated prices cattle that only a short time before were sold only for hides and tallow. He found that he had his own "gold mine" in his ranches and had no need to join the rush to the gold fields of the Mother Lode!

Mariano Malarín residence in Santa Clara, California

CHAPTER VI
UNDER THE AMERICAN FLAG
THE 1850s

The riches engendered by the Gold Rush did not bring peace to Pacheco. The new California immigrants looked with envy at the enormous ranches of the old Californians. Commodore John D. Sloat in 1846 had "guaranteed" their "title" to each estate, and the Treaty of Guadalupe Hidalgo had also recognized the property rights of Mexican Californians. The arriving Americans, however, reasoned that they had won the war, that the natives were a minority, and further, that the grants were illegal. Often self-seeking politicians allied themselves with the squatters and advocated their claims.

The laws delayed the just verification of the land claims of the Californians, subjecting them to lengthy and costly lawsuits which so impoverished many that in the end they lost their land. The Harvard University philosopher Josiah Royce wrote eloquently of the problem of land titles and the resulting "injustice of our treatment of California land owners."[91]

Francisco Pacheco received no better treatment than the rest; however, his recently acquired financial wealth allowed him better to survive the long litigations. He was in a more advantageous position than most of the *rancheros*, whose main assets were cattle and land. After many years, all of the Pacheco ranches were finally confirmed by the United States Federal Courts.

Several attorneys fought Pacheco's suits through the courts. Delos R. Ashley, his principal counsel (who served successively as state assemblyman, state senator, and state treasurer before becoming a congressman from Nevada),[92] set his fee for legal services to Pacheco at $9,500, not an inconsiderable amount. Pacheco was careful to obtain all the legal documents possible to support the claim to his son's Rancho San Luis Gonzaga. For example, he had José Abrego obtain, by payments, certain releases in Mexico City from the original grantee, Francisco José Rivera.

It was many years before final patents were issued for all the Pacheco family ranches: Ausaymas y San Felipe was not confirmed until April 18, 1859; San Justo, December 6, 1865; Bolsa San Felipe, April 10, 1866; Orestimba, July 1, 1870; and San Luis Gonzaga, May 16, 1871[93] San Luis Gonzaga and the Orestimba proved the most difficult; both were at first rejected by the Board of Commissioners, but they were confirmed on appeal.

Before, the San Luis Gonzaga land was confirmed, a lengthy dispute arose over the boundaries. In 1869 Mariano Malarín and

his wife Isidora filed a protest, claiming the 1859 survey of Rancho San Luis Gonzaga by United States Deputy Surveyor James
E. Terrell was in error. The Malaríns declared the notice of the
result of the survey was not legally published, that Pacheco was
ill at that time, and that the owners were not aware of the boundaries. They stated that much of the land in Terrell's survey was
"rocky," "worthless," and inferior to the vacant land to the east
extending to the San Joaquin River, an original boundary. Joaquín Bolado (Bolado Park is named in his honor), who leased San
Luis Gonzaga land in the 1850s, testified the survey could not
have been made in a "worse manner."

The government replied that the survey had been accepted for
ten years and that the lands outside the 1859 survey had been
sold. They further quoted "one Viegas, major-domo" of Pacheco,
who had said in 1859 that the hills had better grazing than the
valley lands. The Malaríns did not succeed in changing the boundaries, and in 1871 President U. S. Grant confirmed the grant,
based on the 1859 survey.[94]

Land claims were not Pacheco's only legal difficulty. In 1856 he
filed suit against the well-known San Francisco businessman
Felix Argenti and J. B. E. Cavallier for not paying $6,648.32 to
the firm of Bolton and Barron, and Pacheco won the judgement.[95]
Pacheco had business transactions with Bolton and Barron, as
shown in his will. James B. Bolton was named as trustee with
Isidora in arranging funds for his grandchildren, and this company also held his Bank of England notes. These two San Francisco merchants, agents for the New Almaden mines, were fluent
in the Spanish language and thus attractive to Pacheco.

Pacheco was also, in these years, harassed by bandits. The San
Francisco Vigilance Committee of 1851 drove many of its most
notorious scoundrels from the city, and it is believed some of
these were the robbers who raided Pacheco's home shortly afterwards. An account, first published years before, appeared in the
Salinas Daily Journal in 1927. According to this article, the
brigands stole about $18,000 in gold.

A vivid description of this affair was given by Jules B. Lombard, Vice-Consul of France, who wrote from Monterey on
January 20, 1851:

"There is in this neighborhood of Monterey a ranchero by the name of Pacheco.
This ex-Mexican officer, established in this county for more than twenty years, had
acquired a very large fortune. Hospitable and good to all unfortunates, never a
single one ever knocked on his door without returning satisfied. Two months ago,
fifteen to twenty Americans presented themselves at his home in broad daylight

and demanded to drink. The good man hastened to satisfy their desires; but they had hardly entered than these bandits grabbed him and his family (women without defense), bound them, locked them up and, pistol on throat, ordered the old man under penalty of death to hand over his money. It was only common sense to submit to such a formulated request. In an instant trunks, chests, boxes, everything was looted, broken into and the band disappeared, taking with them a sum evaluated at more than fourteen thousand piastres (seventy thousand francs) . . . three days later collectors of taxes presented themselves to this same man, ordered him under penalty of immediate sale of his ranch to pay, at that very moment, four thousand and some hundred piastres, the amount of his impositions!"[96]

Following this raid, Pacheco moved his family to his Monterey town house. The American bandits had accomplished what the Indians from the Tulares failed to achieve.

The Monterey home, Casa Pacheco, still stands, greatly modified, at the southwest corner of Abrego and Webster streets. A two-story adobe house of twenty-five rooms, it is one of the largest in Monterey. Amelie Elkinton writes of it: "This Pacheco house was probably the most elaborately furnished in Monterey at the time of Pacheco's death unless the Amesti was equally well done."[97]

Two additional events of interest concerning Pacheco's ranches occurred in 1851. In February there was a brief gold rush to Pacheco Pass. The *Sacramento Transcript* of February 14, 1851, reported that sixty to seventy were mining there, earning from $5 to $9 a day, and some even more.

The same year, 1851, Dr. Pierre Garnier wrote of a curious episode at the ranch.

"Only epidemics of eruptive fevers are reported, such as small pox, which has disappeared since the importation of vaccine or vacuna. I must mention at this point that several rancheros at San Felipe and San Luis in the province of Monterey had discovered cow-pox among their herds and used the vaccine effectively on themselves and their children."[98]

In 1855 Pacheco decided to sell some of his lands. It does not appear likely that a need for cash was a paramount reason for this decision, for his financial condition was indeed sound. In 1851 the Monterey County assessment rolls showed him to be the wealthiest man in the county, and he is listed as owning two homes, one in the town of Monterey, one on his ranch. At the latter he had thousands of head of cattle. Also the rolls recorded his assets at $152,989, of which $50,000 was in cash. This assessment roll did not include his extensive holdings in Santa Clara and Mariposa counties. (At that date, neither Merced County, formed from Mariposa, nor San Benito County, formed from Monterey, had been established.) Pacheco's decision to sell land was probably influenced by squatter problems.

Isaac Mylar, who was living in San Juan Bautista at the time of these first sales, wrote of the squatter troubles. Pacheco, as will be explained later in detail, sold Rancho San Justo to the Bixbys and their associates. Mylar stated that some of the squatters did not leave that ranch for several years and "some of the squatters held hard feelings against the new owners of the land and nourished a grudge against them . . . One credited with being greatly incensed at having to move." This man, Florence Spitts, was so incensed that he killed a brother of Llewellyn Bixby, one of the new owners.[99] It is also recorded that a colony of Mormons, who believed they had settled on government land, were living on the San Junto at the time the rancho was sold.[100]

Rancho San Justo was Pacheco's first sale, completed in 1855. For it he received $25,000. The new owners were Thomas Flint, Benjamin Flint, and Llewellyn Bixby.[101] The Flints and Bixby were cousins who, in 1852, brought a thousand sheep across the plains to California. When Pacheco sold the San Justo, the understanding was that Colonel W. W. Hollister, who had also driven sheep to California, would buy one half of the ranch, which he did.[102]

By 1870, however, only the Flints remained on the ranch. In 1868 Hollister sold his part for $370,000 and moved to Santa Barbara County, where he developed another immense ranch. The Bixbys, who since 1866 had been buying land in Southern California in the area where Long Beach is now located, also left San Justo. The Flint family home, in which they lived for many years, is now a Franciscan retreat house.

The second major Pacheco sale occurred on April 6, 1857, when four square leagues of the Rancho Ausaymus y San Felipe were conveyed to Gustave Touchard, James Dunne, and Peter Dunne.[103] Shortly afterwards, Francisco Pacheco sold one half of the Bolsa de San Felipe ranch to the Dunnes for $5,000.[104] In 1860 James Dunne acquired the interest of both his brother Peter and Touchard, and he continued to acquire other ranches, becoming one of the great landowners of central California. The Pacheco property remained in the Dunne family until 1936, when Franklyn (Frank) O'Connell purchased it. His family still owns this ranch. The names of small settlements recalling the early days often appeared on maps of that region: Dunneville, Pacheco, and San Felipe. None developed, and all have disappeared from recent maps.

Pacheco's son-in-law, Sebastián Núñez, on February 23, 1859 sold a four-fifth interest in the Orestimba grant to Count Leonetto Cipriani, the colorful Italian adventurer who developed the estate at Belmont that was later sold to William C. Ralston. Núñez received for his land $5,800 or twenty-seven cents an acre! Cipriani a few years later sold part of the ranch for three dollars an acre, a tidy profit.[105] Jack Brotherton, the Stanislaus historian, believes Núñez made this seemingly undesireable sale because it took so long to have the ranch patented and the land "had been squattered on by outsiders."

Pacheco's family sorrows were many in the 1850s. In January 1855 his son Juan, the grantee of the Rancho San Luis Gonzaga, died. Two years later, on June 20, 1857, his wife, Feliciana, was buried. Her will, signed by an x, was witnessed by José Abrego, a prominent Mexican-born Californian, who stated her age at death was between 55 and 60 (probably it was 59). The other witnesses were Jacinto Rodríguez, a native Californian who held various offices in Monterey including that of *alcalde*, and Rafael Sánchez, who also had held important positions including that of secretary to Governor Micheltorena. Written in Spanish, the will followed the Spanish style, with long passages testifying to Feliciana Pacheco's Roman Catholic faith. Her husband was made sole executor and sole heir to her estate; however, she directed that certain money be distributed to the poor of Monterey.[106]

Feliciana's will was contested. Máximo Taboas and Buenaventura Núñez filed petitions. Taboas, who had married Encarnación Pacheco, claimed that the property of Feliciana and Francisco Pacheco was communal. California, under Spanish and Mexican law, held that property acquired during marriage was common property of the husband and wife, this in contrast to English (and United States of that period) common law.[107] Encarnación had died shortly after her mother, leaving two children, Manuel and Francisco, and her husband considered her to be one of the rightful heirs.[108]

Buenaventura Núñez, who also contested the will, was the son of Feliciana's daughter Jacinta, who had married Sebastián Núñez in 1841. In replying to Buenaventura's claim, Francisco Pacheco stated that Buenaventura was born in 1836 and was illegitimate. In May 1859 both cases were dismissed, a settlement having been made by Pacheco's attorneys. The *Santa Cruz Pacific Sentinel* reported on June 4, 1859, that this suit "involved the title to more property than any other suit ever brought before the courts of Monterey." Many prominent attorneys from San Francisco, San Jose, Santa Cruz, and Monterey were associated with this case, leading the same newspaper to comment regarding the settlement: "We submit that this looks like throwing the legal profession out of employment."[109]

Also that same year, 1859, Pacheco was again in the courts, sueing the Vallejo family for $3,428. In 1854 the same Máximo Taboas had foreclosed on a mortgage given by a brother of Mariano Guadalupe Vallejo, Juan Antonio. Originally Vallejo owed $6,080, and on October 21, 1857, Taboas assigned the mortgage to Pacheco, there still being $3,416 due which the Probate Court had approved paying. Pacheco brought suit against Mariano Vallejo, who had become executor of the estate after his brother's death in 1857.[110]

Much has been written about the two-story hostelry at the San Luis Station. A number of travelers to the area, among them the 1859 Butterfield Stage passenger Waterman L. Ormsby, mentioned the "hospitable table" and wrote that it was the "only house within thirty miles" and was "a great rendezvous for drovers going into the valley for cattle."[111] A correspondent for the *San Francisco Bulletin* in 1858 also described a meal at the San Luis ranch: "a cup of bean coffee, some stale bread and cold meat."[112] It has been claimed that Francisco Pacheco was the "proprietor" of this "hotel,"[113] but that is not so. Pacheco's health was failing, and he was living in Monterey at this time.

It is usually claimed that this adobe building was destroyed by the earthquake of 1868 and replaced by the wooden building that stood so long near the original adobe with the gun ports. In 1969 the Oakland Museum acquired a watercolor of the "Rancho de San Luis Gonzaga - vista Del Corral" signed "B.L." dated "Setiembre 20, 1857." This interesting painting not only shows the one-story adobe built by Juan Pacheco, but also a two-story wooden building. The wooden building is in accord with Ormsby's description of it as a "country farm house in Connecticut."

It is unlikely that the adobe building was destroyed in 1868, as the earthquake of that year was caused by the Hayward Fault and apparently did not affect the San Joaquin Valley in the region of the San Luis headquarters. The destruction may have been caused by the great earthquake of January 8 and 9, 1857. This earthquake had its center at Tejón, and many believe it was California's greatest in modern times. Another possibility is its destruction by a local earthquake.[114]

Pacheco's relationship with the priests of his church was always one of friendship. This is shown in his actions when applying for his ranches and is reflected in Father Zephyrin Englehardt's works; the Franciscan is quite out-spoken regarding the actions of some Californians, but he is never critical of Francisco Pacheco. An incident in 1856 reflects his friendship. On February 22, 1856, Archbishop Joseph Sadoc Alemany of San Francisco wrote Pablo de la Guerra in Santa Barbara informing him of a visit to Carmel Mission by the pastor of Monterey and Francisco Pacheco to locate the graves of those buried in the sanctuary. They could find nothing because of the rubble.[115] It is most likely that this was an early attempt to find Father Junípero Serra's grave.

Pacheco in 1858 again showed devotion to his church when he assumed the major expense of renovating and enlarging the Royal Presidio Chapel of Monterey, now the San Carlos Cathedral. Monterey's newspaper had moved to Santa Cruz and, as the *Pacific Sentinel*, served as the only newspaper for Santa Cruz and Monterey counties. On January 22, 1859, it reported the January 16th celebration held in Monterey marking the completion of the rebuilding. There was a brass band present, a cannon was fired, and more than two hundred people attended a gala luncheon. The newspaper reported that the cost of the restoration had exceeded $10,000 and noted: "The most liberal and generous donor was Don Francisco Pacheco, a highly respected, venerable Mexican citizen, who has resided in Monterey County nearly forty years and who contributed most efficiently to the completion of the edifice where deceased members of his family now lie buried."[116] This crypt is located below the floor, just outside the sanctuary. A plaque on the floor is inscribed "Pacheco Family - 1858."

The relative obscurity of Francisco Pacheco has led various historians to name the well-known Governor Romualdo Pacheco as the benefactor who enlarged the Monterey Catholic church. Writers of books on the California missions who have erred in this regard include George Wharton James in 1906, Mrs. A. S. C. Forbes in 1909, Rexford Newcomb in 1925, Mrs. Fremont Older in 1938, John Berger in 1941, and Hildegarde Hawthorne in 1942.[117] Mrs. Forbes stated the "Mission" was enlarged "at the order of Governor Pacheco who donated the money."[118] Berger expanded the theme further, claiming "a faithful layman Romualdo Pacheco who later served the unexpired term of Governor Newton Booth donated the funds to enlarge the buildings."[119] The "faithful layman" was in fact buried from St. Paul's Episcopal Church in Oakland by the Masonic Order of which he was a member.[120] Earlier, Father Cayetano Sorrentini, pastor of the Monterey Church related that in 1855 Francisco Pacheco was responsible for two new bells, purchased in San Francisco and placed in the San Carlos Church tower.

As the decade of the 1850s, a period of great change, drew to a close, Pacheco, feeling he was old, decided to "put his house in order."

Isidora Pacheco Malarín, wife of Mariano Malarín

CHAPTER VII
ISIDORA, THE FAVORITE

Pacheco was not old by our present standards, but he considered himself old. He had great affection for his only surviving child, his unmarried daughter Isidora, often called Lola, who resided with him. Pacheco referred to her in his will, written in 1859, with deep appreciation and love. He wrote of her as the one "whom in my old age I have been indebted for much kind care and attention for which I strongly feel and appreciate."

In that same year he decided it was time Lola, now thirty years old and heiress to his fortune, should be married. He chose as an eligible son-in-law Mariano Malarín. Mariano was the son of Juan Malarín, a native of Lima, Peru. Juan Malarín's father, Nicolás Malarín, born in Genoa, Italy, had journeyed to Lima where he married a Spanish lady, Cecilia Girón.

Mariano Malarín, in his interview with Bancroft's agent in 1891, stated that his grandfather's name was originally Malarini, but when he arrived in Peru he dropped the "i." Mariano further related that on a trip to Europe he himself visited relatives in Italy "with the original name of Malarini."[121]

Juan Malarín, who, according to his son, had served first in the Spanish Navy and later in the merchant marine, arrived in California from Peru in 1820 as captain of the ship *Señoriano*.[122] In 1824 he married Josepha Estrada, daughter of José Mariano Estrada and Isabel Argüello. The latter's mother was a Moraga; thus Mariano Malarín was a member of one of the oldest and most aristocratic families of California, a family that included two governors of the state.[123]

Mariano, whose full name was Joseph Mariano Pablo Malarín, was born in Monterey on January 15, 1827, according to his own statements. He attended William Hartnell's school in Monterey and continued when it moved to Alisal (near the present Salinas). After the school closed in 1836 he was sent to Fort Vancouver in the Oregon country to continue his education; however, he found the school there to be merely "one of the Hudson Bay Company's primary schools" and soon returned to California.[124] He was then sent to Lima, Peru, where he had relatives. He stayed there eleven years, and after his graduation from the law school of the University of Lima, he practiced his profession in Lima and taught at the university.

In March 1849 Mariano's father died, and he was recalled to Monterey, California, to become, with his mother, an executor of the estate. Included in the assets were three land grants located in the Salinas Valley, Ranchos Chualar, Zanjones, and Guadalupe.

Mariano served Monterey County in various positions, including judge and supervisor, and was elected a member of the State Assembly in the 10th and 11th sessions of 1859 and 1860. In his first election he defeated R. L. Mathews and E. C. Williams, receiving 62% of the vote. He was elected to a second term by a two-to-one majority over his opponent, M. A. Castro; however, he did not choose to run for a third term.

While serving in the legislature in Sacramento, Malarín sponsored bills which were for the most part of benefit to his Monterey constituents, such as one regulating hogs running at large. However, he also sponsored a resolution requiring that reports from certain officials be printed in Spanish as well as in English.[125]

Malarín's integrity is demonstrated by his vote in April 1860 against the infamous "bulkhead bill." This bill would have given the port of San Francisco to a group of speculators for fifty years. It was the general belief that those voting in favor of the bill, the majority in the Assembly, had accepted favors. With all his ability, Malarín was unable, however, to control his large family, who mortgaged the family ranches at ruinous interest rates and consequently lost them.

A legend persists that the Malarín family was greatly disturbed about his marriage to Isidora Pacheco, but because of her fortune they deemed it necessary. They were of the opinion that their family was socially superior, and that Mariano was sacrificing himself.

Photographs show Mariano Malarín to have been fair skinned and of European appearance, while a photograph of Isidora Pacheco indicates she had a darker complexion and possibly Indian features.[126] Father Englehardt, the Franciscan historian, has written about the distinct classes in California and the upper classes marrying among themselves. Members of this group prided themselves upon their Castilian blood and were usually lighter in complexion than other Hispanic Californians.[127] In general this opinion is shared by a recent writer, David T. Garr.[128]

Whatever the social implications of the marriage of Isidora Pacheco and Mariano Malarín may have been, the wedding took place in the San Carlos Church in Monterey on October 25, 1859. Pacheco's plan for his daughter's marriage to a suitable young man had been accomplished. With his affairs settled, the 70-year-old *ranchero* died a few months later. The Requiem Mass was sung on March 9, 1860, and his body placed in the family crypt he had built in the Monterey church.

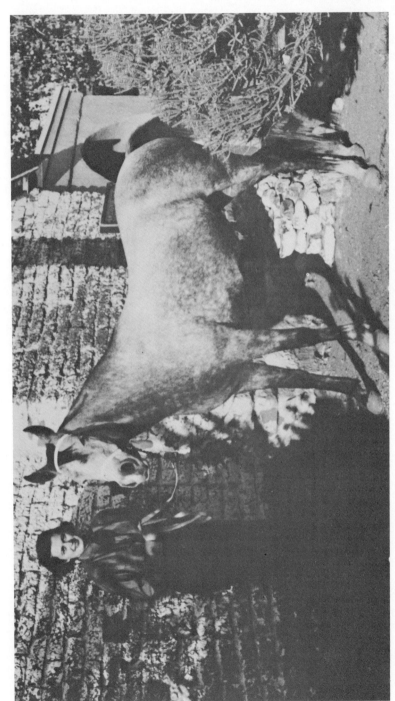

Paula Fatjo and Arabian Mare at San Luis Adobe

CHAPTER VIII
LAST TESTAMENT

Francisco Pacheco's death in 1860 was recorded in the leading newspapers throughout the state. The *Sacramento Union* referred to him as "the wealthiest ranchero of Monterey County" and stated he had made his fortune by his own efforts. The obituary also referred to him as a liberal benefactor of the Catholic Church and recalled his generosity in the renovation of the "old chapel" in Monterey.[129] The *San Francisco Alta California* (May 4 and June 14, 1860) and the *San Francisco Herald* (June 20, 1860) had articles, both giving details of the distribution of his large estate.

Pacheco's will opened with a statement that he was a native of Mexico, now a citizen of the United States. Continuing with a shade of sadness, he wrote that "finding myself advanced in age," he would arrange his affairs "so that at my decease as little difficulty as possible may arise." He then praised his surviving child, Isidora, explaining how he appreciated her kindness to him, "since others, to who I have been a friend and should let my old age pass in quietude, wishing to possess themselves of the fruit of my many years of ceaseless toil, even now when of all the days of my life I most needed repose, have harassed me until I have almost wearied of life."[130]

To his daughter, Pacheco left his Monterey residence and contents and adjoining lots. The horses, carriages, and wagons were also bequeathed to her. Of the remaining estate, he left to his "old and esteemed friend Sebastián Núñez" one fourth and to his daughter Isidora one half. The remaining one fourth went to Isidora and James R. Bolton to be converted into United States bonds and the interest to be paid to Manuel Taboas and Francisco Taboas, minor children of his deceased daughter Encarnación, until they were 21 years of age. If they were to die before reaching that age, the entire investment was to be given to the Roman Catholic Orphanage in San Francisco.[131] If they lived, they were to receive the entire principal at age 21.

Pacheco further wrote: "And whereas Máximo Taboas threatens to claim for himself and his children . . . and to demand an inheritance . . . to avoid suit and trouble in that respect, my heirs shall compromise and pay to the said Máximo Taboas and his children a consideration," but in case this is done "the two eighths of my property herebefore set apart and given to said Manuel and Francisco shall be reduced and made less the amount they shall so recover or be paid in compromise — the benefit of

such reduction being to and for my said daughter Isidora."
Pacheco advised his heirs to resist the claims of the Taboas family and "defend my estate from them . . . not from mercenary or
unworthy motives, but because such claims are unjust and those
making them have worried me and harassed me and had no mercy for my age and want of repose." He appointed Isidora and his
son-in-law Sebastián Núñez executors. The document was signed
February 18, 1859.[132]

Pacheco's estate was appraised at $234,516.50, a large fortune
at that time. It included seven lots in the city of Monterey, the
"Rancho San Felipe containing 17,748 acres," valued at $35,496.
The ranch house and the corrals of the San Felipe were valued at
$3,500. Rancho San Luis Gonzaga contained over 48,000 acres
and had a value of $18,302.63; its improvements were valued at
$2,000. The Rancho Bolsa of San Felipe had a value of $18,311.[133]

The *ranchero's* personal estate, including the household fur-
niture, was valued at $84,504.63. Listed were such items as a
piano, five family portraits,[134] a picture of the ranch house, eigh-
teen pistols and other guns of various types, six gold watch
chains, two lumps of gold "about 16 oz.," one bag of gold dust
weighing about sixteen ounces, silver-mounted saddles, carriages, mules, chickens, and fifteen tame cows, to name a few of
the items. Among those owing him money were the Dunnes and
Gustave Touchard ($11,125.00), while a note of Domingo
Danglada for $1,000 was marked on the inventory as "valueless."

At the Rancho San Felipe, the animals included hogs, horses of
various types, tame cows, 4,400 head of stock cattle, 1,100 ewes,
1,600 lambs, 700 "younger ones," and 700 wethers (castrated
rams). The entire inventory filled seven pages. The final items
were his notes of the Bank of England, recalling the time when
these notes were considered the soundest investment in the
world. The inventory was signed by his executor and executrix,
Sebastián Núñez and Isidora Pacheco de Malarín.[135]

Among the claims presented to the estate was that of his
physician, Dr. J. D. Callaghan, for $1,178; however, the doctor
owed the estate about the same amount. There were also bills
from local merchants for a gold watch and chain $140, two velvet
mantillas $95, a China shawl $100, eighty-three fruit trees, $48,
and twenty-eight posts $7, to name a few items. The funeral cost,
submitted by Father Juan Comellas, was $1,500. The property
tax for the Rancho San Luis Gonzaga, paid to Merced County,
was $63. It is certainly an amazing contrast to the present unjust
taxation of Merced County, which has failed to protect its open

32

spaces and ranch lands by refusing to adopt the Williamson Act as most enlightened counties have.

Pacheco also left a library. Bancroft recorded that "there were three or four libraries in California, other than those of the missions, being M. G. Vallejo's at Sonoma, Hartnell's, which had cost him a good sum, and from which he readily lent to his friends, Francisco Pacheco's collection was worthy of notice, consisting as it did of *periódicos empastados*, and books on Mexican history." According to Bancroft, "Pacheco's went into possession of his brother-in-law [sic] Mariano Malarín of Santa Clara."[136]

Under the capable management of Núñez and Malarín, the other heirs received their legacies, and the estate was distributed March 3, 1862. This distribution included four lots in San Juan Bautista not in Pacheco's inventory. Francisco Pacheco had not judged wrongly in his selection of Mariano Malarín as the spouse for his favorite child.

CHAPTER IX
EPILOGUE

The Malaríns survived the terrible drought years of 1863 and 1864 which saw so many California ranches lost. Isaac Mylar, in his recollections, related how on the Pacheco ranch there was a slough that led into Soap Lake. In 1864 this slough, he wrote, was "lined with decaying carcasses of cattle, who too weak to pull themselves out of the mud, died there . . . They died by hundreds whilst striving to reach some tule or some wisp of grass that they saw growing on the banks of the slough."[137]

William Brewer, a Yale professor, led a surveying party to explore and chart California in the 1860s. He visited the San Luis Gonzaga ranch and crossed Pacheco Pass in 1862. Two years later, during the drought, he again was on the ranch and has left a vivid description of that disastrous year.

"May 30, we came to the San Luis de Gonzaga Ranch . . . our road lay over the mountains. They are perfectly dry and barren, no grass . . . here and there a poor cow is seen, but what she gets to eat is very mysterious . . . . Dust fills the air . . . it covers everything . . . . All around the house it looks desolate. Where there were green pastures when we camped here two years ago, now all is dry, dusty, bare ground. Three hundred cattle have died by the miserable water hole back of the house . . . and their stench pollutes the air.

This ranch contains eleven square leagues. . . . In its better days it had ten thousand head of cattle, besides the horses needed to manage them. Later it became a sheep ranch and two years ago . . . it fed sixteen thousand sheep besides some few thousand cattle. Now owing to the drought, there is no feed for cattle and not over one thousand sheep, if that, can be kept through the summer. The last of the cattle, about one thousand head, were lately sold for $1,500 or only $1.50 each! Such is the effect of the drought on one ranch.[138]

Dr. Robert Glass Cleland, in *The Cattle on a Thousand Hills*, sums up the disaster: "The thousands of head of black cattle and beasts of burden, which once carried the familiar brands of the proudest of California families, disappeared forever from the plains and valleys and rolling hills."[139] The Malaríns survived, however, and left the Pacheco ranches intact.

In the 1860s Malarín and his family moved from Monterey to Santa Clara. The "old Pacific Capital" had become a city of quiet and, to quote Augusta Fink, "the halcyon days of political prestige and commercial expansion were over."[140] Malarín explained that his move to the San Jose area was made "on account of legal matters and so I could attend the federal courts . . . and then I had a good many relatives there." He continued: "I had a terrible lot of litigation with squatters and others as to the title to the land. Mostly with the United States surveyor and his deputies who always decided in favor of the squatters. The United States did not treat us fairly." Malarín also declared, "I gave my cases to [Henry W.] Halleck of San Francisco." He further reported that through "bad surveys I lost at this time over 1,100 acres of land," and that he would lose 300 acres more because the "United States surveyor had mixed things so badly."[141]

For a few years Malarín himself occupied the Pacheco ranch adobe during the summer months. The *Hollister Free Lance* of December 24, 1886, stated:

> The old adobe mansion is perhaps one of the most attractive buildings in the country. The long wide veranda, its open portals, its thick and lasting walls . . . It has stood for years, and apparently will last for ages. Mr. Malarín repaired it thoroughly a few years ago. During the summer months the family make it their home and to hear and witness the merry making, one could easily imagine he was living in the land of the sunny vine . . . . The orchard contains almost every variety of fruit, the vineyard which was laid out a few years ago is doing remarkably well, the olive trees are strong and hardy.[142]

By 1889 the Gillespies occupied the Pacheco adobe, so it appears Malarín built his own large wooden residence about that time. This house, located near the old adobe, was later moved eastward to the Víboras Creek area. After the death of Malarín it became the residence of his son-in-law Dr. Ramón Roca. Around 1906 Dr. Roca sold the San Felipe ranch to T. S. Hawkins, the pioneer San Benito banker and rancher. The Hawkins family still owns this ranch, but the Malarín-Roca home was demolished in 1976.

Malarín, after his move to Santa Clara, continued his career as a distinguished member of the bar. He also became president of the San Jose Safe Deposit Bank of Saving, associated with the well-known bankers John E. Auzerais and Edward McLaughlin. This long-successful bank was sold in 1917 to the Bank of Italy, predecessor of the Bank of America. Malarín remained president of the bank until his death on April 28, 1895. His wife, Lola (Isidora), had died in 1892 and was the last of the Pacheco family to be buried in their vault in the San Carlos Cathedral in Monterey.

The Malaríns were parents of six children; however, only two daughters survived their parents. One was their eldest daughter, Paula, who in 1888 married Dr. Luis Fatjo of Barcelona, Spain. They had probably been introduced by the Antoine Fatjos of

Santa Clara. When the Malaríns moved to Santa Clara, one of the reasons given for the move was the "good many relatives there."[143] Across from the Malarín residence lived Antoine Fatjo, who had married Mariano's sister Refugio.[144] Dr. Luis Fatjo was a graduate of the Medical Department of the University of Barcelona, licensed to practice in California in 1891. Shortly after Paula's marriage, her sister Mariana also married a graduate of the medical school in Barcelona, Dr. Ramón Roca, who was licensed to practice in California in 1892.

In his will, Mariano Malarín bequeathed to his daughter Mariana Malarín de Roca the 17,752-acre Rancho Ausaymas y San Felipe and an additional 1,600 acres in San Benito County. His other daughter, Paula Malarín de Fatjo, received the Rancho San Luis Gonzaga, containing 48,281 acres in Santa Clara and Merced counties.[145] As the new century approached, the Pacheco family, represented by a new generation, still owned a vast domain in Central California.

Francisco Pérez Pacheco belied the stereotype of the nineteenth-century Mexican Californian. "The Mexicans," Jonathan Green wrote in 1829, "will neither work themselves nor are they willing that foreigners should be more industrious."[146] A few years later in 1846 Lieutenant F. A. M. Craven, of the United States Navy, wrote of "the state of utter degradation" to which the Mexican Californians were reduced.[147] *The Annals of San Francisco*, published in 1855, described the "Hispano-Americans" as "ignorant and lazy."[148]

This attitude prevailed even in 1875 when James Denman, San Francisco Superintendent of Schools, declared the inhabitants during the Mexican era "were not elevated in the scale of intelligence above the flocks they herded."[149] The well-known historian Theodore Hittell observed: "If visited upon their ranchos, they were sure to be found lying in the shade, smoking cigarritos or drinking aguardiente."[150]

The lives of Francisco Pacheco and his distinguished decendants certainly refute these "American Images of Spanish California," to use Dr. Hart's appropriate description.[151] That Pacheco's wife could not write is not unexpected. Hartnell's suggestion in Monterey in 1835, "Let our daughters also be educated," was considered a "revolutionary proposal."[152] Nor was illiteracy confined to Hispanic California at that time. Thomas Larkin wrote of the Americans he knew in a section of the eastern United States he was residing in during the 1820s:

"One fourth can not write and one half can not write more than their name."[153]

The portrait of Francisco Pacheco by Leonardo Barbieri depicts him as a dignified gentleman of quiet strength and intelligence. These qualities were proved. Pacheco overcame all obstacles and became a leading personage in California. Pacheco Pass can be proud of the name it bears, a name of distinction in the annals of our state.

NOTES

1   Joseph Warren Revere, **A Tour of Duty in California** (New York & Boston: C. S. Francis & Co., 1849), pp. 43-45, 104, 105.

2   St. Aloysius, as the saint is called by the English-speaking world, was a Jesuit, a member of the Gonzaga family, Dukes of Mantua.

3   Donald C. Cutter, "The California Franciscans as Anthropologists," **The Masterkey**, vol. 34, no. 3 (1960), pp. 88-94.

4   S. F. Cook, "Conflict Between the California Indians and White Civilization," in **California Indians**, ed. R. F. Heizer (Berkeley: University of California Press, 1952), p. 473.

5   Ogden Hoffman, **Reports of Land Cases Determined in the United States District Court for the Northern District of California**, vol. 1 (San Francisco: Numa Hubert, Publisher, 1862; reprint ed., Buffalo, N.Y.: Dennis & Co., Inc., 1966), p. 114.

6   References to Frémont in Ferol Egan, **Frémont** (New York: Doubleday and Company, 1977), p. 323; and in Fred B. Rogers, **Montgomery and the Portsmouth** (San Francisco: John Howell, 1958), p. 69. References to Sutter in Hubert Howe Bancroft, **History of California**, vol. 4 (San Francisco: The History Company, 1886), pp. 486-487.

7   Francis P. Farquhar, ed., "The Topographical Reports of Lieutenant George H. Derby," **California Historical Society Quarterly**, vol. 11, no. 2 (June 1932), p. 103.

8   Remi Nadeau, **The Real Joaquín Murieta** (Corona del Mar, Ca.: Trans-Anglo Books, 1974), pp. 74, 82.

9   L. A. Norton, **Life and Adventures** (Oakland, Ca.: Pacific Press Publishing House, 1887), pp. 315-317.

10 **Murieta and Vasquez** (Hollister, Ca.: Evening Free Lance, 1927), p. 8.

11 H. H. Bancroft, **Bancroft's Guide** (San Francisco: H. H. Bancroft & Co., 1872), p. 48.

12 Andrew S. Hallidie, "Ho! For the Kern River," manuscript (circa 1853) in the California Historical Society Library, San Francisco.

13 Pat Adler and Walt Wheelock, **From Walker's R.R. Routes - 1853**, (Glendale, Ca.: La Siesta Press, 1965), p. 13.

14 Zoeth Skinner Eldredge, **History of California**, vol. 4 (New York: The Century History Company, 1915), p. 403.

15 Carl I. Wheat, **Mapping the Trans-Mississippi West**, vol. 4 (San Francisco: The Institute of Historical Cartography, 1960), pp. 79, 90, 148-149.

16 William N. Abeloe, **Historic Spots in California**, 3rd ed. (Stanford: CA. Stanford University Press, 1966), p. 202.

17 Records of the Bureau of Land Management (Record Group 49), Microfilm T910, "California Private Land Claim Dockets." Includes "correspondence, maps, original documents, and reports on private land claims." Federal Archives and Records Center, 1000 Commodore Drive, San Bruno, California.

18 Waterman L. Ormsby, **The Butterfield Overland Mail** (San Marino, Ca.: Huntington Library, 1942), pp. 123-124.

19 Robert J. Braud, Chairman, Santa Clara Transportation Action, refers to this highway as the "Pacheco Pass death trap" in the **San Francisco Examiner**, December 10, 1976..

20 John Muir, **A Thousand Mile Walk to the Gulf** (Boston & New York: Houghton Mifflin Company, 1916), pp. 189-190.
21 **Sacramento Union,** July 18, 1860.
22 Bancroft, **History of California,** vol. 4, p. 763.
23 Ibid., vol. 2, p. 263.
24 Baptismal Records, San Carlos Cathedral (formerly Royal Presidio Chapel), Monterey, California.
25 Feliciana Pacheco's Will, Probate –91, Monterey County Court House, Salinas, California.
26 Copy of original Petition, dated November 6, 1826, in the Santa Barbara Mission Archives.
27 Bancroft, **History of California,** vol. 4, p. 763.
28 Ibid., vol. 2, p. 763.
29 Pacheco's November 6, 1826, Petition.
30 Amelie Elkinton, "A Monterey Expedition Against Rebel Indians," **Noticias del Puerto de Monterey,** vol. 6, no. 2 (June 1962), p. 6.
31 Augusta Fink, **Adobes in the Sun** (San Francisco: Chronicle Books, 1972), p. 84.
32 Interview by Ralph Milliken with Fernando Zanetta in 1928. Copy of the interview given to the author personally by Ralph Milliken.
33 Isaac Mylar, **Early Days at Mission San Juan Bautista** (Watsonville, Ca.: Evening Pajaronian, 1929), p. 188.
34 Malarín Dictation, 1891, in the Bancroft Library, University of California, Berkeley.
35 Bancroft, **History of California,** vol. 2, pp. 527-537.
36 Ibid., p. 532.
37 Ibid., p. 536.
38 City Records, Monterey, California. "Grants," vol. A, p. 14½.
39 Personal letter from Amelie Elkinton.
40 Pacheco's November 6, 1826, Petition.
41 Copy of Father Sarría's letter in opposition, dated December 18, 1826, from the original in the Santa Barbara Mission Archives.
42 Copy of Governor Echeandía's statement, dated January 16, 1827, from the original in the Santa Barbara Mission Archives.
   Rancho Tularcitos was granted in 1834 to Rafael Gómez.
43 Bancroft, **History of California,** vol. 3, p. 36.
44 Ibid., p. 136.
45 Ibid., p. 74.
46 Baptismal Records, San Carlos Cathedral, Monterey, California.
47 Bancroft, **History of California,** vol. 4, p. 763.
48 Ibid.
49 Ibid., vol. 3, pp. 672-673.
50 George L. Harding, **Zamorano** (Los Angeles: The Zamorano Club, 1934), p. 80.
51 Ibid.
52 Susanna Bryant Dakin, **Lives of William Hartnell** (Stanford, Ca.: Stanford University Press, 1949), p. 208.
53 Charles E. Chapman, **A History of California — The Spanish Period** (New York: The Macmillan Company, 1921), pp. 466-473.
54 Andrew F. Rolle, **California, a History,** 2nd ed. (New York: Thomas Y. Crowell Company, 1969), p. 304.

55 Report in the California State Archives, Sacramento.
56 Maynard Geiger, O.F.M., **Franciscan Missionaries in Hispanic California** (San Marino, Ca.: Huntington Library, 1969), p. 19.
57 Ralph Milliken, **The Padre and His Pools**, a one-page sketch (Los Banos, Ca.: Chamber of Commerce, 1967).
58 Ausaymus was said to have been the name of an Indian chief, but it probably means "Indian people," according to Santa Clara's historian Clyde Arbuckle.
59 Tracy Storer and Lloyd Tevis, Jr., **California Grizzly Bear** (Berkeley: University of California Press, 1955), pp. 18, 118.
60 Hoffman, **Reports of Land Cases**, vol. 1, Appendix, p. 9.
61 Ibid.
62 Ibid., Appendix, p. 10.
63 Barry M. Gough, ed., "Views of Lt. George Peard, R.N., on Alta California," **Southern California Quarterly**, vol. 56, no. 3 (Fall 1974), p. 224.
64 George P. Hammond, ed., **Larkin Papers**, vol. 2, 1843-1844 (Berkeley: University of California Press, 1952), p. 14.
65 Bancroft, **History of California**, vol. 3, p. 513; and Donald M. Craig, ed., **William Robert Garner — Letters from California** (Berkeley: University of California Press, 1970), p. 23.
66 Hoffman, **Reports of Land Cases**, vol. 1, Appendix, p. 10.
67 Abeloe, **Historic Spots in California**, p. 312.
68 Hoffman, **Reports of Land Cases**, vol. 1, pp. 113-114.
69 Ibid., pp. 113-116.
70 Bancroft, **History of California**, vol. 4, p. 471.
71 Abeloe, **Historic Spots in California**, p. 203; and A. L. Kroeber, **Handbook of the Indians of California** (Washington, D.C.: Government Printing Office, 1925), p. 444.
72 Abeloe, **Historic Spots in California**, p. 312.
73 Mission San Carlos Records, Entry 1122.
74 Ibid., Entry 4535.
75 Hoffman, **Reports of Land Cases**, vol. 1, p. 191. A creek in western Stanislaus County still bears the Indian name Orestimba.
76 Ralph Milliken, **Los Banos Enterprise**, October 21, 1968.
77 Original Larkin Account Books, 1841-1847, Bancroft Library, University of California, Berkeley.
78 Richard Dillon, **Fool's Gold** (New York: Coward-McCann, 1967), pp. 168-169.
79 Bancroft, **History of California**, vol. 4, pp. 486-487.
80 Letter in the collection of Dr. Dudley Bennett, San Francisco. Sutter used this spelling of "New Helvetia."
81 Bancroft, **History of California**, vol. 4, pp. 407, 652, 661, 662.
82 "The Prominent Men of California in 1846," **Pacific Monthly**, vol. 10 (August 1863), p. 151.
83 Thomas S. Martin, **With Frémont to California and the Southwest, 1845-1849**, ed. Ferol Egan (Ashland, Oregon: Lewis Osborne, 1975), p. 17.
84 Craig, ed., **William Robert Garner**, pp. 170-171.
85 Capt. Daniel D. Heustis, **Remarkable Adventures of Captain Daniel D. Heustis in California**, ed. by Carey S. Bliss (Los Angeles: Glen Dawson, 1957), pp. 5-6.
86 William Heath Davis, **Seventy-Five Years in California**, ed. Harold A. Small (San Francisco: John Howell, 1967), p. 283.
87 Chester S. Lyman, **Around the Horn to the Sandwich Islands and California 1845-1850**, ed. Frederick J. Teggart (New Haven: Yale University Press, 1924), p. 243.

88 Gillespie's recollections appeared in 1965 in the **Hollister Free Lance**. Gillespie was born in San Felipe in 1885 and with the aid of his mother wrote an account of the adobe.

89 Etienne Derbec, **A French Journalist in the California Gold Rush**, ed. A. P. Nasatir (Georgetown, Ca.: The Talisman Press, 1964), p. 95.

90 Hammond, ed., **Larkin Papers**, vol. 7, 1847-1848, pp. 28, 29, 39.

91 Josiah Royce, **California from the Conquest in 1846 to the Second Vigilance Committee of San Francisco** (Boston & New York: Houghton Mifflin Company, 1886), pp. 467-494.

92 Ashley is also remembered as the father-in-law of the California poet Dan O'Connell.

93 Robert G. Cowan, **Ranchos of California** (Fresno, Ca.: Academy Library Guild, 1956), pp. (in order of the final patents for the ranches listed) 17, 82, 75, 55, 83.

94 Records of the Bureau of Land Management (Record Group 49), Microfilm T910, "California Private Land Claim Dockets."

95 Document in the California Historical Society Library, San Francisco.

96 Jules B. Lombard, "A French Pessimist in California," trans. A. P. Nasatir, **California Historical Society Quarterly**, vol. 31, no. 3 (September 1952), p. 259.

97 Personal letter from Amelie Elkinton.

98 Doyce B. Nunis, **A Medical Journey in California by Dr. Pierre Garnier** (Los Angeles: Zeitlin & Ver Brugge, 1967), p. 59.

99 Mylar, **Early Days at Mission San Juan Bautista**, pp. 41-42.

100 James Miller Gwinn, **History and Biographic Record of Monterey and San Benito Counties**, vol. 2 (Los Angeles: Historic Record Co., 1910), p. 325.

101 Monterey County Records, Salinas, California, Vol. B, "Deeds," October 2, 1855. Also John Hayes, "Farming in the Pajaro Valley," **Overland Monthly**, October 1870, p. 349.

102 **Diary of Dr. Thomas Flint** (Los Angeles: reprinted from the Annual Publications of the Historical Society of Southern California, 1923), p. 75.

103 Federal Court Records, Bancroft Library.

104 Ibid.

105 Stanislaus County Records, courtesy of Jack Brotherton.

106 Feliciana Pacheco's Will.

107 Donald E. Worcester, "The Significance of the Spanish Borderlands to the United States," **Western Historical Quarterly**, vol. 7, no. 1 (January 1976), p. 11.

108 A third child, Esteban, had died.

109 **Santa Cruz Pacific Sentinel**, June 4, 1859.

110 Juan Antonio Vallejo's estate included Monterey town lots and the Rancho Bolsa de Cayetano near Watsonville.

111 Ormsby, **The Butterfield Overland Mail**, p. 122.

112 Walter B. Lang, **The First Overland Mail** (San Marino, Ca.: Huntington Library, 1942), p. 14.

113 R. P. Conkling and M. B. Conkling, **Butterfield Overland Mail**, vol. 2 (Glendale, Ca.: The Arthur H. Clark Company, 1947), p. 296.

114 U.S. Department of Commerce, **Destructive and Near Destructive Earthquakes in California and Western Nevada**, Special Publication, No. 191 (1934). Also, **San Francisco Alta California**, January 8, 12, 13, 18, 1857; **Los Angeles Times**, January 21, 1962; **California Geology**, vol. 25, no. 8 (August 1972).

115 Personal letter from Rev. Maynard Geiger, O.F.M., quoting the Archbishop's letter of February 22, 1856.

116   **Santa Cruz Pacific Sentinel,** January 22, 1859.

117   George Wharton James, **In and Out of the Old Missions** (Boston: Little, Brown and Company, 1906).
      Mrs. A. S. C. Forbes, **California Missions and Landmarks** (Los Angeles: 1935) p. 229.
      Rexford Newcomb, **The Old Mission Churches and Historic Houses of California** (Philadelphia & London: J. B. Lippincott Company, 1925).
      Mrs. Fremont Older, **California Missions and Their Romances** (New York: Coward-McCann, Inc., 1938).
      John A. Berger, **The Franciscan Missions of California** (New York: G. P. Putnam's Sons, 1941).
      Hildegarde Hawthorne, **California Missions** (New York: D. Appleton-Century Company, 1942).

118   Forbes,

119   Berger, **Franciscan Missions of California,** p. 282.

120   Peter T. Conmy, **Romualdo Pacheco** (San Francisco: Native Sons of the Golden West, 1957), p. 14.

121   Malarín Dictation, 1891.

122   Bancroft, **History of California,** vol. 4, p. 728.

123   José Darío Argüello, Governor, 1814-1815; and Luis Antonio Argüllo, Governor, 1822-1825.

124   Malarín Dictation, 1891.

125   Reports of the State Treasurer, State Controller, and State Superintendent of Public Instruction, January 19, 1860. Malarín's bills are in the State Archives at Sacramento.

126   Photograph from the collection of Paula Fatjo.

127   Zephyrin Englehardt, **Missions and Missionaries of California,** vol. 3 (Santa Barbara, Ca.: The Arthur H. Clark Company, 1929), p. 130.

128   David T. Garr, "A Rare and Desolate Land: Population and Race in Hispanic California," **Western Historical Quarterly,** vol. 6, no. 2 (April 1972), pp. 147-148.

129   **Sacramento Union,** July 18, 1860.

130   Francisco Pacheco's Will, Probate –107, Monterey County Court House, Salinas, California.

131   This was the first Catholic Orphanage in California, then located on Market Street where the Palace Hotel now stands. Founded in 1851, it had opened under the Sisters of Charity in 1852.

132   Francisco Pacheco's Will.

133   Ibid.

134   These most likely were the oil paintings by the artist Leonardo Barbieri, now owned by Pacheco's great-granddaughter Monserrat Roca of Santa Clara.

135   Francisco Pacheco's Will.

136   Bancroft, **History of California,** vol. 34, **California Pastoral** (San Francisco: The History Company, 1888), p. 523. Larkin's "Account Books" list Pacheco as buying a copy of the **History of Columbia** in 1841.

137   Mylar, **Early Days at Mission San Juan Bautista,** p. 141.

138   William H. Brewer, **Up and Down California,** ed. Francis P. Farquhar (New Haven: Yale University Press, 1930), pp. 508-509.

139   Dr. Robert Glass Cleland, **The Cattle on a Thousand Hills, Southern California 1850-1880** (originally published, 1941; reprint ed., San Marino, Ca.; Huntington Library, 1975), p. 137.

140 Augusta Fink, **Monterey, The Presence of the Past** (San Francisco: Chronicle Books, 1972), p. 122.
141 Malarín Dictation, 1891.
142 **Hollister Free Lance,** December 24, 1886.
143 Malarín Dictation, 1891.
144 María Refugio Malarín, born August 3, 1840, had first married her cousin David Spence, II, and after his death, Antoine Fatjo.
145 **San Francisco Examiner,** May 4, 1895.
146 Jonathan S. Green, **Journal on the North-West Coast of America in the Year 1829** (New York: Chas. Fred. Heartman, 1915), pp. 104-105.
147 John H. Kemble, ed. **Naval Campaign 1846-1849, Journal of Lieutenant Tunas Augustus MacDonough Craven, U.S.N. United States Sloop of War** *Dale* (San Francisco: The Book Club of California, 1973), pp. 52-54.
148 Frank Soulé, John Gihon, and James Nisbet, **The Annals of San Francisco** (New York & San Francisco: D. Appleton & Company, 1855), pp. 53, 471.
149 James Denman, speech at the dedication of the new building of Boys' High School, November 15, 1875, San Francisco.
150 Theodore H. Hittell, **History of California,** vol. 2 (San Francisco: Pacific Press Publishing House, 1885), p. 471.
151 James D. Hart, **American Images of Spanish California** (Berkeley: Friends of the Bancroft Library, 1960).
152 Dakin, **Lives of William Hartnell,** p. 209.
153 Robert J. Parker, ed., **Chapters in the Early Life of Thomas Larkin** (San Francisco: California Historical Society, 1939), p. 11.

INDEX

Compiled by
Anna Marie and Everett Gordon Hager

Forbes, Mrs. A. S. C., 26
Fort Vancouver, 28
Frémont, John Charles, 2; at Gavilán
   Peak, 17

− G −

Garner, William Robert, 12, quoted, 17
Garnier, Pierre, 22
Garr, David T., 29
Gavilán Peak, 17
Geiger, Fr. Maynard, quoted, 11
Gillespie, Chester G., describes
   adobe, 18
Gilroy, 1, 2
Gómez, Fr. Manuel, 5
Gonzáles, José Theodoro, 5
Gonzáles, y Torres, Feliciana,
   see Pacheco, Feliciana
Grant, U. S., 21
Green, Jonathan, quoted, 36
Guerra, Pablo de la, 26
Gutíerrez, Nicolás, 12

− H −

Halleck, Henry W., 2, 35
Hallidie, Andrew S., 3
Haro, Francisco de, 8
Hartnell, William, 10, 28
Hawkins, T. S., acquires San Felipe, 35
Hawthorne, Hildegarde, 26
Heustis, Daniel D., quoted, 17-18
Hill's Ferry, 2
Hittell, Theodore, quoted, 36
Hollenbeck, William, 3
Hollister, W. W., 23
Hollister Free Lance (newsp.), 35

− J −

James, George Wharton, 26

− K −

Kearny, Stephen, W., 2
Kern River, 2, 3

− L −

Laguna San Felipe, see Soap Lake
Larkin, Thomas O., 12; praises Pacheco,
   16-17; naval agent, 18; 36-37
Leese, Jacob, signs bond, 18
Leidesdorff, William A., signs bond, 19

Lima, Peru, 28
Lombard, Jules, B., 21
Los Angeles, made capital, 10
Los Baños, 1, 2, 11
Los Baños del Padre Arroyo
   (Menjoulet Canyon), 11
Love, Harry, 2
Lyman, Chester S., quoted, 18

− Mc −

McLaughlin, Edward, 35

− M −

Malarín, Isidora (Lola) Pacheco, 21,
   28-30; legacy, 31; executrix, 32;
   death, 35
Malarín, Joseph Mariano Pablo
   (Mariano), 7, 20, 28-30 **passim**;
   capabilities, 33, drought faced, 34;
   death, 35; bequests, 36
Malarín, Juan, 10; death, 28
Malarín, Mariana, see Roca, Mrs. Ramón
Malarín, (Malarini), Nicolás, 28
Malarín, Paula, see Fatjo, Mrs. Luis
Malarín, Refugio, see Fatjo,
   Mrs. Antoine
Marshall, James, 19
Martin, Thomas S., 17
Mathes, Michael, 6
Mathews, R. L., 29
Mejía, José María, 14
Menjoulet Canyon, 11
Micheltorena, Manuel, 1, 14;
   defenses, 16; 24
Mission Carmel, 8
Mission San Carlos, 8
Mission San Juan Bautista, 11
Mission Santa Barbara, 8
Mission Santa Inés, 8
Monterey, a pueblo, 5, 6, 8, 9, 10, 21;
   Pacheco home in, 22; restoration of
   Presidio Chapel, 26
Moraga, Gabriel, 1, 14
Muir, John, quoted, 4
Murieta, Joaquín, 2
Mylar, Isaac, 23, 24

− N −

Nadeau, Remi, quoted, 2
Native Sons of the Golden West, 15
Newcomb, Rexford, 26

45